MORBID LUMINOSITY

M.B.B. Whyte

Dedicated to Ed for completely destroying my original concept by giving me an even better one. Thanks for the extra work!

M.B.B. Whyte

First Edition
ISBN-13: 978-0-692-92859-2
ISBN-10: 0-692-92859-6

Contact: Email: mbbwhyte@gmail.com

CONTENTS

MORBID LUMINOSITY

M.B.B. Whyte

,

FLOWER

A smiling flower sways
as the wind blows gently.

Soft petals wave
at the neighboring weeds.

It's beauty glows
amid the surrounding dirt.

I stomp on it
to make it fit in.

AGAINST THE CURRENT

My thoughts,
flow like water,
cleansing,
purging the demons.

They swim
against the current,
struggling.

This is a fight
they must win.

FEAR OF DROWNING

Thunder crashes
and you scurry
under a tree.

Cowardly,
you shiver,
draped in darkness,
afraid of harmless raindrops.

Suddenly,
the sky goes black
and the rain pours down.

Dodging the raindrops
you go on,
afraid to stop
for fear of drowning.

I'M ALIVE

I scratch
myself a blister,
the pain
splitting open the skin.

Cracked
and bleeding,
the sting
is comforting.

It reminds me
that I am alive.

FAME

a poet
smothering in the spotlight
of fame

having sex
among the poems
of hate and fear
bitterness and loathing

it's a lonely place
but is it worth it?

A MUCH NEEDED REST

This page is my escape route.
But, reality is not an ink refill.

It is but the pen
that has just run out;
you can barely see it,
but the imprint is there.

If I had an eraser
I could make the ink disappear.

I would have to rub
really hard
and may rip the paper.

Then I would have to start over.

And I don't want to do that.

ALONE AND LONELY

A lonely man
walks briskly,
arms swaying,
staring aimlessly;
avoiding the decay
surrounding him.

Nameless faces
blur into one another,
creating a blob of burning skin
that melts away,
exposing the truth.

He smells the stench
of painted ladies
and three-piece suits
as they try to
cover up the disintegration.
Behind their smiles?
Fangs,
waiting for the comfort
and security
of darkness
to reveal themselves.

Meaningless voices

whisper from
all directions,
as he catches
a reflection
in a passing window.

He must hurry to shelter
for it is
almost nightfall.

NORMALITY

Normalcy;
a vague delusion,
as erratic
and polluted thoughts
swirl in gray matter
held in by delicate obstructions.

THE ART OF CONCERN

I have perfected the art of concern.
Tell me a sad story;
I'll shed a tear on cue.
An underrated performance;
I am an imposter,
spewing empathy from my lips.
"Feeling better?"
"How's the family?"
"Sorry for your loss."
"blah, blah, blah."
But, it is apathy
that resides
behind my eyes
And, you are clueless,
unaware and unable
to accept the truth.

INSIGNIFICANCE

On a cold, dark December night
sheltered in a warm blanket
I am comfortable
and at ease

COMFORT

Let me borrow
your mouth,
a place to rest my tongue.
The words balance gently
on my lips,
betrayed by emotion,
a promise sealed;
a promise broken
with a kiss.

The familiar
taste of security
blinded to the past,
wrongs righted
with just a soft caress.

DEPRESSION

Driving down
like a knife through bone,
this sharp,
unyielding feeling
grates at my existence.

It tugs
like an unwilling dog
on a leash.

The self-inflicted wounds
that grace my mind
will not heal.

Instead, they become
more infected
with every thought,
every betrayal

Every misguided,
trusting word.

REGRET

Regret
never stops bleeding,
no matter how much time
is applied.
Frailty
keeps the wound open.
The burden,
keeps the memories
gushing forth.

STILL

Shadowed,
in the remains of still,
life and love
are immortal.

Reminiscences
are future manifestations.

The almost
becomes warped actuality.

Imagined memories
never manifest,
only replay over again
ignored by reality.

MY CURRENT STATE OF MIND

What can you say
when all words
have been spoken?

The seeds of lust
do not always
grow into
flowers of love.

Impending fate
always
tears the heart
apart.

Don't dream.
Don't breathe.
Stay still.

Don't wake me.
I need to spend
more time wallowing.

Collecting my dreams,
saving my sorrows,
in my secret place.

MORTALITY

Love,
being mortal,
may itself,
one-day die.

Or,
like a temperamental woman,
change without warning.

And,
in doing so,
destroy the spirit
and dissolve faith.

M.B.B. Whyte

EMPTINESS (POEM IN PROGRESS)

Heart ripped out
through skin and bone
hanging by a vein
pumping desperately
until the binding snaps
and the blood flows freely
putting an end to the fatigue.
It's tired now
It wants to rest.

REBIRTH

Alone,
like the first rose
of spring,
I come into life
an infant.

I struggle
and fall,
only to be
reborn
at the first sign
of light.

JUSTICE

Time does not
heal all wounds.
Some fester and
simmer slowly
waiting for the perfect
moment to resurface.

MOOD

discontented
crawling through the moments
with no particular destination

FADE

Memories in color
fade to gray
as they take their place
on the top shelf
of eternity,
Out of sight.
Out of mind.
for safe keeping.

FREEDOM

The mind
needs to roam.
It cannot
be left on a chain
in the yard,
with only
a bowl of food
in which to feed.

THE FROST

Grasping hands
of desolation
cling to the trees
for life.
The living,
trapped under ice,
dig their way out
with frostbitten minds.

HIERARCHY

The upper class
sit upon their thrones,
viewing their subjects
then switching channels.

They sit,
drinking,
burping insults
and tossing the empties
into someone else's yard.

They congregate
to create laws
that damn the starving
and chop off the heads
of the motivated.

They rule a dormant society
ready to erupt.

Until, one day,
they awaken
to a steaming hot cup
of realization;
their tongues stained

with the blood
of self-inflicted indignities

HIGH SCHOOL OUTCAST

Closet Goth,
the black hidden behind closed doors.
Bauhaus, Joy Division and Siouxsie
kept me company when the outside world
refused to understand.
The blanket of indignation and dejection
kept me warm when the frigid air
of normalcy became too much to bear.
For these were not my peers.
They were sunshine disciples,
sycophants to the king of conformity.
And I was disparate,
discontented
and couldn't be bothered.

UNTITLED

Jesus called today –
He was stressed out
and needed to vent.
He said
He wished there were
more non-believers,
He's under enough pressure
as it is.

I SAW TOMORROW

I saw tomorrow
standing next to me.
Staring, glaring
through distant eyes.
It motioned me to stay,
but I just couldn't wait.

I saw tomorrow
right in front of me
holding out the hand of fate.
It was shaking slightly,
so I touched it gently.
Then it turned away.

I saw tomorrow
walk away from me,
fading silently into the dawn.
I tried to catch it,

but I lost it in the wind,
never to see it again.

INTRUDERS

The laughing cries
of children
playing kickball
on the sweating asphalt,
intrude my thoughts.

Their voices
sing in the faint breezes.

Their smiles
sail towards my room.

I close the window
so they can't get in.

JEALOUSY

Jealousy,
grown up,
still acts like a child
when he doesn't get his way.

Left unattended,
kicking and screaming,
his feelings spread
like cancerous cells
until he cries himself
to sleep.

THE ENCHANTRESS

The enchantress'
vigilant eye
looks after the moon
like a protective mother.

The moon
welcomes her embrace
as the darkness,
intimidating and emphatic,
closes in;
threatening to beset
the light in shadow.

The Conflict
tempers nightly
until the light,
drained and weary,
succumbs to the morning.

LIFECYCLE

Life
And Death;
the impartial fragments
of time.

The intermediate –
A struggle
with deceptive expectations
of the outside
pseudo-world.

Dysphoria
breathes peaceful resignation
in perpetual darkness
awaiting departure

INSOMNIA

Like an unwanted guest,
night intrudes.
Ignoring him,
I stare at the ceiling;
each crack a stretch of road
laid before me.
Each stain,
a reminiscence,
playing over and over
like a broken record.
The silence,
loud as a jackhammer,
awakens dormant voices.
The sunlight.
Interrupts the moment,
searing the morning into my eyes.

MOVING ON

Leaning my head
on the window,
the train speeds
steadily to its destination.

My eyes dart sharply
as I watch the trees
and buildings fly by.

Each leaf
a teardrop ready to fall
and every brick
a heart waiting to crumble.

All I see,
is a memory
that vanishes from my mind
as quickly as they do
from my sight.
But the pain
isn't worth a few
scattered memories.

The further I go,

the quicker
the images fly by.

Blurred by the speed
of the moving train.

OBSESSION

You are in my head,
trampling through
on your way home;
your footsteps
embedded in my soul.

You speak to me
at night
when it is quiet
and I am alone.
The dark;
a mutual friend.

Your voice,
a rusty nail,
pierces my heart
and I am infected.

In your words
I feel your hurt.
Through my skin
they are absorbed,
becoming part of me.

In your words

I feel your death,
but they cannot
extinguish the fear.

The fear
of what is inside
eternally burning.

The fear
that I am hopeless;
succumbing
to my own illusions.

NIGHT FANTASY

As night gently caresses my heart
wiping the day away,
I have seen this face
a million times,
my prelude to sleep.

I delve into persuading eyes
that dance along
to his sultry song.

Around me
his voice wraps,
warming the unsympathetic darkness.

I slip slowly into slumber
as he falls from my fantasy.

WINTER'S DESTRUCTION

The last leaves disappear
into the wind,
to an unknown destination.

The last petal falls
to the ground,
to be buried in the frost.

The last sunray
loses its life,
and is covered by the clouds.

And I,
descend
into the dark
and bitter bite of the cold.

A SINGLE BLACK ROSE

There is beauty in a black rose
not seen by the naked eye.
A unique strangeness
felt by the heart.

It radiates
only in the night
like a lonely firefly.

The day cannot comprehend
its mysteriousness

It confuses,
as does the wind,
swirling dry leaves
around you
as you walk.

It baffles,
as does
the meaning of life,
anyone who may encounter it.

Its existence proves one thing:
there is beauty, even in darkness.

THE SNOWFLAKE DANCE

In the moonlight
the snowflakes dance.

I catch one,
and the cold sensation
dying on my tongue,
revives memories
I am not ready
to discard.

I am here
alone,
frightened.

Afraid
the pictures may fade.

Afraid
they will be forgotten.

In the moonlight
the snowflakes laugh.

They will melt
and yet I shall remain;
holding on

afraid to let go.

STRIFE

Driving to work
each day,
I watch
the dead flying ant
decompose
on my dashboard.

M.B.B. Whyte

STALLED

Green light

car stalls
engine turns over
battery dies.

dumbfounded
and helpless

passing cars
speeding by
beep angrily

THE SUPERMARKET

The world
is a black hole,
sucking you deeper and deeper
into the pit of aggravation.

I am the abused,
the stepped on;
the peon.

Yet,
still, I smile
and say, "thank you."

My nerves are shot
and my head aches.

I can't hold on
much longer.
Am I the cause
of all suffering
on this planet?

The black hole
will only expand
until I explode.

No!
You can't have that
for the sale price
and there are no rain checks.

If you don't like it,
go to another store.

PERSPECTIVE

Sitting in the cheap seats,

looking down at the front row
dancing in their superiority
as they snub their noses,

I observe, laughing.

From up high,
I can see all.

They
can only see
what is front of them.

SLEEP

Under the cover of darkness
confusion stalks
my dreams
always a step ahead
of the coming day.

UTOPIA

Sinking in a sigh
my thoughts blur.
A dream-like cloud
covers my eyes
and I squint
to see through the haze.
The forms
are familiar shadows,
bathed in moonlight,
waltzing to a song
composed by Orpheus himself

They dance joyously.
as the night
wraps around them,
passing with knowing smiles;
laughing,
as Diana shields them
from Apollo's emergence

They remain,
clinging to the night
As the haze
lifts from my eyes;
my thoughts focus

and I awaken.
I blink
and they are gone

THE WATCHER

Bitter tree limbs
grow out of the dry,
cracked Earth,
barren from the summer heat.
Fingers wickedly point,
scolding a lost generation;
Standing in judgment,
looking down on us,
as if it were our fault
that it stands isolated
and alone.

STARLIGHT

Glimmering

Solitary

The Brightest Star
basks in its magnificence

As nearby stars
shun its brilliance

REALITY

Sorting through the crap
that resides in my subconscious,
separating fact from fiction
is burdensome.

The fiction is comforting,
bearable,
welcoming
seductive,

Reality is exasperating.
The real world,
unacceptable.

TABLOID FODDER

Yesterday's headlines,
forgotten by today,
fade into obscurity;
leaving a few scant truths
of your insignificance behind

REFLECTION

Fatalists are not born.
They are created,
by the uncreative,
the egotistical,
the hypocritical,
the naysayers,
the believers.

They are a product of their environment.

Want to know who is to blame?

Look in the mirror.

ATTENTION

Hate
Love

Positive
Negative

Drama
Harmony.

You absorb the limelight.
As long as the spotlight
is on you

THE IDIOT

A person in love
is like a banana
left out to ripen;
then forgotten
on the kitchen table.

WEDDING BLISS

The prisoner's final rites
were read to him
and he nodded
with an understanding
"I do."

The alcohol is not a comfort
yet, I take another sip.

Commitment is not a celebration.

It is condemnation.

And, what is the cost?
An empty wallet
and an empty heart.

I am committed to myself.
That is a task in itself.

I finish my drink.

Staring at the empty glass,
I cut myself off.

OVER POPULATION

Too many people,
corroded by conceit,
trample through the China shop
refusing to pay
for what they knock over.

POETRY

The poet
wears his heart
on the page,
as he seals his immortality
with every word written

His world,
a story to tell
on the blank page.

His reality,
waiting to be created
with a stroke of the pen.

NIGHTTIME SONG

Alone,
10:30 pm,
speakers
shed acoustic tears
in small quiet sobs.

The soothing voice,
singing of sadness
and longing,
comforts
the anguish of the day.

LATE NIGHT THOUGHTS

Boredom.
Fear of nothing.
Fear of no love,
to give or take.
Fear of hopelessness
and no forgiveness
of past sins.
Fear of hope,
And what it means.
Fear of myself
and the darkness
I am capable of.

Am I a noble person?
Or, am I an aberration,
set upon this earth
to inflict hurt on all
around me.

LIVING

Mortality reveals
the beauty
in even
the most appalling
and grotesque.

Roadkill,
sprawled across the roadway,
becomes a catalyst
for the future.

The bird,
fallen from the nest,
unable to fly;
liberates the inhibitions
from tomorrow.

The gravel on the street,
the new bedspread,
a stranger's glance,
become majestic.

The new car,
nose piercing,
sex;

the little things,
unimportant yesterday
can no longer wait.

1ST IMPRESSION

Strangers walk past,
flip a glance
and in a second
develop an impression
of who they think I am.

How do they know!
I haven't even figured
it out myself.

APATHY

Apathy is the teddy bear
I snuggle with in the night.

Old and tattered,
fur soiled,
body ridden with holes of empathy.

It keeps me warm and safe
I cannot stand to throw it away.

EVERYDAY

Held here
against my will,

$16.00 an hour;
a burden
impossible to shed.

The 9 to 5 grind
invading
my time.

There are bills to pay:
car
phone
utilities

Debts to settle.

Grudges to hold,

keeping me grounded
to this existence.

THE END

The sun collapses;
blackness prevails

God is dead
and His disciples
wander meaninglessly

The others rejoice,
for in his death,
their responsibility has been lifted

M.B.B. Whyte

PUBLICATION CREDITS

"A Single Black Rose" and "The Snowflake Dance" first appeared in the January 2000 edition of The Eagles Flight

"Wedding Bliss" and "Winter" first appeared in Volume Two, Issue Two 2000 of Bleeding Hearts

"Depression" first appeared in the January 2003 edition of Bleeding Hearts

"Jealousy" and "Moving On" first appeared in Issue 67 of The Iconoclast

M.B.B. Whyte

ABOUT THE AUTHOR

MBB Whyte is just a Goth, Metalhead, New Waver, Rivethead, Indie chick who writes shit.

She resides in the 4th largest city in the state of New York where she is fascinated with Pop Culture, watches too much TV, has multiple pretend boyfriends, and is constantly annoyed.

Friends describe her as 'Gen X'er', 'Misanthrope' and "Stalker'.

She lives in her parents' basement with her temperamental Shih Tzu, Cookie, who likes to bite people.

For updates, please visit her blog at www.apsychobabbles.com.

Facebook at https://www.facebook.com/apsychobabbles/

And don't forget Twitter and Instagram!

Twitter: @apsychobabbles
Instagram: @apsychobabbles

M.B.B. Whyte

NOTES AND POETRY

M.B.B. Whyte

MORBID LUMINOSITY

M.B.B. Whyte

MORBID LUMINOSITY

M.B.B. Whyte

MORBID LUMINOSITY

M.B.B. Whyte

MORBID LUMINOSITY

M.B.B. Whyte

MORBID LUMINOSITY

M.B.B. Whyte

MORBID LUMINOSITY

M.B.B. Whyte

MORBID LUMINOSITY

M.B.B. Whyte

www.ingramcontent.com/pod-product-compliance
Lightning Source LLC
Chambersburg PA
CBHW070536030426
42337CB00016B/2228